MVFOL

WORLD'S WEIRDEST
REPTILES

by M.L. Roberts

WATERMILL PRESS

HEY, BIG FELLA

THE GREEN IGUANA

Lizards can be pretty large animals. And the green iguana is one of the largest! This big guy can grow up to 6 feet (1.8 m) long.

A green iguana has a flap of skin, called a dewlap, on its throat. It also has spines running down its back and tail. These protect the iguana from enemies and also make it look attractive to other iguanas.

Green iguanas live in Latin America, where it is hot and wet. They are lazy animals. A good day for an iguana involves lying on a tree branch or near a river bank. When an iguana gets hungry, it munches on some fruit, flowers, and leaves.

What's an iguana's best weapon? Its tail! A green iguana's tail can be several feet long. A swing of that heavy tail can be a painful experience for any enemy that gets too close!

WHAT A SHOWOFF!

THE FRILLED LIZARD

At first glance, there's nothing very special about the frilled lizard. But when this animal is threatened, an amazing change occurs. By tightening some muscles connected to its tongue, the lizard opens a colorful frill around its neck. This makes the mild-mannered lizard look like a ferocious monster. And that's usually enough to scare away most animals.

But what if the animal refuses to take the hint? Then the frilled lizard really gets mad! It will jump at its enemy and bite it. If that doesn't work, the lizard usually decides enough is enough. It will turn around and quickly run away.

Frilled lizards live in Australia and New Guinea. They like to climb trees and eat beetles and spiders.

Most lizards crawl along on all four legs. But the frilled lizard has a faster way to travel. It stands on its back legs and runs so quickly that only three of its four toes touch the ground.

A KNIGHT IN SCALY ARMOR

THE HORNED LIZARD

Is it a lizard or a toad? This short, lumpy creature looks so much like a toad that many people call it just that—a horned toad. But it is really a member of the lizard family.

Horned lizards live in the deserts of North America. Like all reptiles, this animal is cold-blooded and has to soak up warmth from the sun. But if a lizard gets too much sun, it can die—not from a bad sunburn, but because its body gets too hot. So a lizard might slip into a shady spot or dig a hole to lie in until it cools off.

During the day, horned lizards plod across the sand and rocks, looking for insects to eat. They think ants are a real treat!

The spikes on a horned lizard's body protect it from enemies. But it has a weird way to scare off predators—it squirts blood from its eyes! Sounds like a character in a horror movie, doesn't it?

REAL-LIFE DRAGON?

THE KOMODO DRAGON

Scientists used to laugh at stories that dragons really existed. Then, in 1912, they discovered the Komodo dragon. This huge lizard can be found only on Komodo and a few other small islands in Indonesia.

While the Komodo dragon doesn't breathe fire, it's still pretty impressive. In fact, Komodo dragons are the largest member of the lizard family. They can be 10 feet (3 m) long and weigh up to 365 pounds (164 kg)! One lizard is longer than the Komodo dragon, but it is not as heavy.

Of course, a big animal like the Komodo dragon has a big appetite. These animals can run down wild pigs and small deer and swallow them whole!

A Komodo dragon's forked tongue is its most important sense organ. The dragon flicks its tongue in and out all the time to pick up tastes and smells in the air around it.

STICK AROUND!

THE GECKO

How would you like to be able to walk on walls and ceilings? You could if you were a gecko! This little lizard has pads on its toes. Each pad is covered with thousands of tiny hairs that stick to surfaces and help the gecko hang on.

There are more than 750 different types of geckos. They live in warm areas all over the world. Most geckos are active at night. They scurry around, gobbling up insects.

You could say that geckos named themselves. They make a funny noise that sounds like "Gecko! Gecko!" This sound became the little lizard's name.

Some species of geckos have no eyelids. So how do they keep their eyes clean and moist? They stick out their long tongues and lick their eyeballs!

WATER WALKER

THE BASILISK

This little lizard is a real speed demon! Basilisks stand on their hind legs and run as fast as 8 miles (12 km) per hour. Because they move so fast, they can run on top of water! Flaps of skin between its toes also keep the basilisk from sinking.

Like many lizards, a basilisk has bright-colored skin and a crest on top of its head. These features make basilisks attractive to other members of the species.

A monster in Greek mythology that had the head of a rooster and the body of a snake was called a basilisk. Modern scientists thought this lizard's head looked like a rooster's, so they named it after the legendary creature.

THE BIG SQUEEZE

THE EMERALD TREE BOA

Emerald tree boas live in the tropical forests of South America. This snake likes to curl up around the branch of a tree, where it lies hidden in the leaves. It looks as harmless as a bunch of bananas. But as soon as an animal or bird comes too close, these "bananas" become quite deadly. With lightning speed, the boa snatches the animal and coils its long, heavy body around its victim.

Many people think boas crush their victims to death. Not true! This powerful snake actually squeezes its victim so tightly that the animal can't breathe. It dies from suffocation.

In case you're wondering why the emerald tree boa in this picture isn't green (the color of emeralds), it's because this snake is just a baby. Emerald tree boas are red when they are born. As they grow older, they turn yellow and, finally, emerald green.

HI, SPIKE!

THE HORNED SAND VIPER

This snake loves to sunbathe. But it isn't trying to get a tan. Like all reptiles, snakes are cold-blooded. Their body temperature is the same as the air outside. So snakes have to soak up a lot of sun to keep themselves warm.

Sand vipers usually eat small animals, birds, and lizards. A viper has long fangs in the front of its upper jaw. It uses them to grab its prey. But those fangs are the only teeth the viper has! Because the viper can't chew its food, it has to swallow its dinner whole. That's quite a mouthful!

How can a snake swallow an animal that is much bigger than itself? The secret is in its jaw. The two sides of a snake's jaws can move separately, and a snake's lower jaw is only loosely attached to its upper jaw. So the snake can stretch its mouth open wider . . . and wider . . . and WIDER! Gulp!

A MASTER OF DISGUISE

THE VEILED CHAMELEON

This odd-looking creature is brown, the same color as the branch it is standing on. But if you moved it somewhere else, it might turn a totally different color! Chameleons change color in response to changes in light or temperature. They also change when they are frightened or upset. The more excited or angry a chameleon is, the brighter it will be.

Chameleons are not "party animals." In fact, they spend almost their whole lives by themselves. It may sound like a lonely life, but it's what a chameleon likes best.

Chameleon eyes are pretty weird. They're shaped like cones, with only a small opening for the pupil. And each eye can move separately. This means they can look at two different things at the same time!

FAST FOOD!

THE HORNED CHAMELEON

If the ability to change color or to look at two things at the same time isn't weird enough for you, how about having a tongue long enough to shoot out and catch passing insects?

A chameleon's tongue can be several inches long—in fact, the same length as its body! Most of the time, a chameleon keeps its tongue curled up in the back of its mouth. But powerful muscles in a chameleon's throat sends its tongue flicking out faster than the eye can see, snagging an insect flying by. Now that's fast food!

Those spikes sticking out of the horned chameleon's face are handy weapons in a fight. Male chameleons might fight over territory or over a female chameleon. But these fellows are usually pretty peaceful. They're more likely to puff out their throats and bodies to scare each other away than to actually hurt each other.

STICKING YOUR NECK OUT

THE SOFT-SHELLED TURTLE

Ready to go snorkeling? This soft-shelled turtle certainly has the nose for it! A soft-shelled turtle lives on the muddy bottoms of rivers and lakes. By holding its long nose above the water, it can breathe while it swims. A soft-shell can also breathe oxygen from the water and stay submerged for hours at a time.

Most turtles have hard shells. But the soft-shelled turtle's feels—you guessed it!—soft. Actually, its shell is made of bone covered with soft, thick skin.

Turtles are part of a family called chelonians. Chelonians can live a long, long time. It is not uncommon for some turtles and their larger relatives, the tortoises, to live well over 100 years!

You might think the soft-shelled turtle has no way to defend itself without a hard shell for protection. But if you tangled with one of these reptiles, the turtle would probably win! A soft-shelled turtle has strong jaws, sharp claws, and a bad temper. What a grouch!

CARE FOR A BITE?

THE GAVIAL

Imagine having a mouth 4½ times as long as it is wide. It may sound awkward, but that's exactly the kind of snout a gavial has. This animal has such long, thin jaws that its teeth don't fit in its mouth. They stick out the sides of its jaws even when its mouth is closed!

Gavials live in Asia. They like to lie in the water of lakes and rivers. When a fish swims by—snap! Those long jaws come in handy!

Gavials, like their crocodile relatives, lay 40 or more eggs at a time. The mother gavial buries her eggs in the sand, where they'll be warm and safe. When the young hatch, they are only about 15 inches (38 cm) long. But they'll be at least 20 feet (6 m) long when they're all grown up!

CARE FOR A SWIM?

THE MONITOR LIZARD

emember our friend, the Komodo dragon? He is part of the monitor lizard family. There are about 30 different types of monitor lizards.

Many monitor lizards live near water, and they are excellent swimmers and divers. A monitor moves smoothly through the water by weaving its body and tail from side to side.

A monitor lizard is active during the day. It will eat almost anything, from fish to insects to birds. Some monitors are only 8 inches (20.3 cm) long, but most are larger—about 4 feet (1.2 m). The longest, the Salvadori monitor of Papua New Guinea, can be up to 15 feet, 7 inches (4.75 m) long! Obviously, these big lizards aren't afraid of too many things, but they do have to watch out for crocodiles—and people!

A monitor lizard is pretty tough. And if it's cornered, it can be even tougher. A monitor will puff up its body so it looks much larger than it really is. If that doesn't scare its enemy away, the monitor might defend itself by swinging its whiplike tail or biting with its sharp teeth. Ouch!

ARE TWO HEADS BETTER THAN ONE?

THE SHINGLEBACK LIZARD

Wouldn't it be funny if you could avoid a fight just by sticking out your tongue? It works for the shingleback lizard! When this little reptile faces an enemy, it opens its mouth, hisses—and then sticks out its gray and blue tongue! The other animal is so surprised that it backs off or runs away.

Shinglebacks are part of a family of lizards called skinks. There are about 900 species of skinks, and they live in warm places all over the world. The shingleback lives in Australia. It got its name because the scales on its back lay on top of each other, just like the shingles on the roof of a house.

It's hard to tell which end is which on a skink, because its head and tail look a lot alike. This confuses its enemies, who can't figure out which end of the skink to attack. It just goes to show you that two heads are better than one!

BEWARE!

THE GILA MONSTER

True to its name, this lizard looks like something from an old monster movie. And it's dangerous, too. The Gila (HEE-lah) monster and its cousin, the Mexican beaded lizard, are the only poisonous lizards in the world. A bite from a Gila monster can kill an animal, and can be very painful to a person.

Gila monsters live in the southwestern part of the United States and northern Mexico. They spend most of their lives buried in the ground, but come out at night to eat. Because a Gila monster moves very slowly, it has to eat eggs and young animals that are easy to catch.

Gila monsters don't have to worry about finding food every day. This lizard's thick tail is full of fat. If there's nothing to eat, the Gila monster can live off this fat for a long time.

Gila monsters look like they're covered with black and orange beads. But this colorful lizard isn't trying to win any beauty contests. Its bright color warns its enemies that the lizard is poisonous and will make a deadly snack.

Index

Page numbers in **bold** indicate photograph.

Asia, 24
Australia, 4, 28

basilisk, 12, **13**
boa, 14, **15**
body color, 12, 14, 18, 20, 30
body temperature, 6, 16, 18

chameleon, 18, 20
chelonian family, 22
    life span of, 22
crest, 12
crocodile, 24, 26

desert, 6
dewlap, 2

eggs, 24, 30
emerald tree boa, 14, **15**
eyes, 10, 18

food, 2, 4, 6, 8, 10, 14, 16, 20, 24, 26, 30
frilled lizard, 4, **5**

gavial, 24, **25**
gecko, 10, **11**
Gila monster, 30, **31**
Greek mythology, 12
green iguana, 2, **3**

horned chameleon, 20, **21**
horned lizard, 6, **7**
horned sand viper, 16, **17**
horned toad, 6

iguana, 2
Indonesia, 8

Komodo, 8
Komodo dragon, 8, **9**, 26

Latin America, 2
lizard, 2, 4, 6, 8, 10, 12, 26, 28, 30

Mexican beaded lizard, 30
Mexico, 30
monitor lizard, 26, **27**

movement, 4, 10, 12, 26, 30

New Guinea, 4
North America, 6

protection from enemies, 2, 4, 6, 20, 22, 26, 28, 30

reptile, 6, 16, 22, 28

Salvadori monitor lizard, 26
shingleback lizard, 28, **29**
skink, 28
snake, 14, 16
    jaw of, 16
soft-shelled turtle, 22, **23**
South America, 14

tongue, 8, 10, 20, 28
tortoise, 22
turtle, 22

United States, 30

veiled chameleon, 18, **19**
viper, 16

Library of Congress Cataloging-in-Publication Data
Roberts, M.L., (date)
    World's weirdest reptiles / by M.L. Roberts.
        p.   cm.
    Summary: Describes some of the more unusual reptiles, including the gecko, the chameleon, the Gila monster, and the emerald tree boa.
        ISBN 0-8167-3229-9 (lib.)   ISBN 0-8167-3221-3 (pbk.)
        1. Reptiles—Juvenile literature.   [1. Reptiles.]   I. Title.
    QL644.2.R63   1994
    597.9—dc20   93-8493

Printed in the United States of America.
10 9 8 7 6 5 4 3 2 1

Photo credits:

All photos courtesy of Tom Stack & Associates: Photos on pages 3 and 21 ©1994 by Kevin Schafer, pages 5, 7, 29, 31 ©1994 by John Cancalosi, page 9 ©1994 by Denise Tackett, pages 11 and 13 ©1994 by Gary Milburn, page 15 ©1994 by David G. Barker, pages 17 and 19 ©1994 by Brian Parker, page 23 ©1994 by Joe McDonald, page 25 ©1994 by Nancy Adams, page 27 ©1994 by Mike Severns.

Cover photo ©1994 by Gary Milburn.